Lent Bible Stories for Kids 2025

Daily Devotions to Teach Faith Love and the Meaning of Easter

Justin Jackson

Copyright @ JUSTIN JACKSON 2025

All rights reserved. No part of this publication may be reproduced, stored in a retrieval system, or transmitted in any form or by any means—electronic, mechanical, photocopying, recording, or otherwise—without prior written permission from the publisher, except for brief quotations in reviews or articles.

Table Of contents

Introduction...5
    Welcome to Lent: What Is Lent and Why Do We Celebrate It?.. 5
    How to Use This Devotional as a Family............ 6
    Understanding the Journey from Ash Wednesday to Easter... 8

Week 1: Preparing Our Hearts for Lent................... 10
(Ash Wednesday - First Sunday of Lent)................. 10
    Day 1 – Ash Wednesday: A Clean Heart for God. 10
    Bible Story: God Made Us................................ 10
    Scripture: Genesis 2:7, Psalm 51:10................. 10
    Day 2 – Jesus Gets Baptized: A Fresh Start.... 14
    Bible Story: Jesus' Baptism............................. 14
    Scripture: Matthew 3:13-17...............................14
    Day 3 – Jesus Says No to Temptation.............. 17
    Bible Story: Jesus in the Wilderness................ 17
    Scripture: Matthew 4:1-11................................. 17
    Day 4 – The Calling of the Disciples.................22
    Bible Story: Jesus Chooses His Friends...........22
    Scripture: Matthew 4:18-22...............................22
    Day 5 (First sunday of lent) – Loving God with All Our Heart... 26
    Bible Story: The Greatest Commandment........ 26
    Scripture: Matthew 22:36-40.............................26

Week 2: Learning About God's Love (Second Week of Lent) 30
- Day 6 – Zacchaeus: Jesus Loves Everyone 30
- Bible Story: Jesus Meets Zacchaeus 30
- Scripture: Luke 19:1-10 30
- Day 7 – Helping Friends Find Jesus 35
- Bible Story: The Paralyzed Man is Healed 35
- Scripture: Mark 2:1-12 35
- Day 8 – Feeding the Hungry 38
- Bible Story: Jesus Feeds 5,000 People 38
- Scripture: John 6:1-14 38
- Day 9 – Loving Our Enemies 42
- Bible Story: Jesus Teaches About Love 42
- Scripture: Matthew 5:43-48 42
- Day 10 – A Thankful Heart 46
- Bible Story: The Grateful Leper 46
- Scripture: Luke 17:11-19 46
- Day 11 – The Prodigal Son Returns Home 49
- Bible Story: A Father's Unfailing Love 49
- Scripture: Luke 15:11-32 49
- Day 12 (second sunday of lent) – God's Love Never Fails 54
- Bible Story: Nothing Can Separate Us from God's Love 54
- Scripture: Romans 8:38-39 54

Week 3: Jesus Teaches Us About God's Kingdom (Third Week of Lent) 57
- Day 13 – The Beatitudes: Blessings from Jesus .. 57

Bible Story: Jesus Teaches on the Mountain....57
Scripture: Matthew 5:1-12..............................57
Day 14 – Be a Light for Jesus...........................62
Bible Story: A Lamp on a Stand........................62
Scripture: Matthew 5:14-16..............................62
Day 15 – The Good Samaritan: Loving Others.65
Bible Story: Helping Those in Need..................65
Scripture: Luke 10:25-37.................................. 65
Day 16 – The Mustard Seed: Growing in Faith.70
Bible Story: Faith Like a Tiny Seed...................70
Scripture: Matthew 13:31-32.............................70
Day 17 – Building Our Lives on Jesus..............73
Bible Story: The Wise and Foolish Builders......73
Scripture: Matthew 7:24-27...............................73
Day 18 – Trusting Jesus in the Storm...............77
Bible Story: Jesus Calms the Storm................. 77
Scripture: Mark 4:35-41................................... 77
Day 19 – God Cares for Us.............................. 82
Bible Story: Do Not Worry, God Provides......... 82
Scripture: Matthew 6:25-34...............................82

Week 4: Walking with Jesus to the Cross (Fourth Week of Lent).. 85

Day 20 – Palm Sunday: Jesus Enters Jerusalem. 85
Bible Story: The Triumphal Entry......................85
Scripture: Matthew 21:1-11...............................85
Day 21 – Jesus Cleans the Temple.................. 89
Bible Story: Jesus Teaches About True Worship.. 89

Scripture: Mark 11:15-17... 89
Day 22 – The Last Supper: Jesus' Special Meal.. 93
Bible Story: Jesus Shares Bread and Wine......93
Scripture: Luke 22:14-20................................. 93
Day 23 – Jesus Washes His Disciples' Feet.....97
Bible Story: A Lesson in Serving Others...........97
Scripture: John 13:3-17..................................... 97
Day 24 – Jesus Prays in the Garden.............. 100
Bible Story: Jesus in Gethsemane..................100
Scripture: Matthew 26:36-46...........................100
Day 25 – Jesus is Arrested and Betrayed...... 105
Bible Story: Judas and the Soldiers................ 105
Scripture: Luke 22:47-53................................ 105
Day 26 – Jesus Stands Before Pilate............. 109
Bible Story: Jesus is Put on Trial.................... 109
Scripture: Matthew 27:11-26...........................109

Holy Week: Jesus' Journey to the Cross............... 114

Day 27 – Good Friday: Jesus Dies on the Cross.. 114
Theme of the Day: The Great Sacrifice: Jesus Shows His Love... 114
Bible Story: The Crucifixion............................114
Scripture: Luke 23:33-49.................................114
Day 28 – The Day of Waiting (Holy Saturday) 120
Theme of the Day: Waiting with Hope: The Promise of New Life..120
Bible Story: Jesus is Buried............................ 120
Scripture: Matthew 27:57-66...........................120

Easter Sunday: Jesus is Alive!............................ **125**
    Theme of the Day: The Greatest Miracle: Jesus Is Alive!... 125
    Bible Story: The Resurrection......................... 125
    Scripture: Matthew 28:1-10............................ 125
Conclusion... **130**
Bonus Chapter.. **132**

Introduction

Welcome to Lent: What Is Lent and Why Do We Celebrate It?

Lent is a special time of year when we take a journey with Jesus. Starting on Ash Wednesday and leading up to Easter Sunday. These days remind us of the time Jesus spent in the wilderness, fasting and praying before beginning His ministry (Matthew 4:1-11). Just like Jesus prepared His heart for the work God had for Him, Lent is a time for us to prepare our hearts for Easter—the day we celebrate Jesus' victory over sin and death! During Lent, Christians all over the world take time to pray, read God's Word, and grow closer to Jesus. Some people fast, which means giving up something they enjoy, like sweets or screen time, to focus more on God. Others choose to do something extra, like helping those in need or spending more time in prayer as a family. But Lent isn't just about giving things up—it's about growing in faith. It's about making room in our hearts for Jesus and remembering how much He loves us. It's a time to slow down, to listen, and to reflect on what Jesus did for us on the cross. When Easter finally arrives, our hearts will be ready to celebrate with great joy because we will have spent these days drawing closer to our Savior!

How to Use This Devotional as a Family

This devotional is designed to help your family walk through Lent together in a way that is simple, meaningful, and fun! Each day, you will find:
- A Theme – A special focus for the day that helps us think about Jesus and His love for us.
- A Bible Verse – God's Word to guide us and help us grow.
- A Reflection – A short and easy-to-understand devotional that includes a story or example to help kids and adults connect with the message.
- A Prayer – A way to talk to God as a family and invite Him into our journey.

-    An Action Step – A fun challenge or activity to help live out what we learned.

This devotional is meant to be a simple and joy-filled part of your day. You can read it together at breakfast, before bedtime, or during family prayer time. If you have young children, you can ask them questions and let them share their thoughts. If your kids are older, you can challenge them to dig deeper into the Bible.

Remember, Lent is not about being perfect—it's about growing closer to Jesus. Some days might be busy, and you might miss a reading, but that's okay! What matters most is that your family takes time to focus on Jesus and His incredible love.

Understanding the Journey from Ash Wednesday to Easter

Lent is like a big adventure—a journey that leads us closer to the heart of Jesus. Along the way, we will explore important moments from the Bible, learning about:

- Ash Wednesday – A day to remember that we belong to God and that we need His grace every day.
- Jesus in the Wilderness – How Jesus trusted God during hard times and how we can do the same.
- Parables of Jesus – Stories that Jesus told to teach us about God's kingdom.
- The Last Supper – The meal Jesus shared with His disciples before He went to the cross.
- Good Friday – The day Jesus gave His life for us, showing the greatest love of all.
- Easter Sunday – The best news ever! Jesus is alive, and His love never ends!

Each week of this devotional will help us think about who Jesus is, why He came, and how we can follow Him. By the time Easter morning arrives, our hearts will be full of faith, joy, and love for our risen Savior! So, are you ready to begin this journey? Let's walk with Jesus, listen to His words, and let His love change our hearts. Lent is here—let's make it a time of growing, learning, and celebrating the amazing love of God!

Week 1: Preparing Our Hearts for Lent

(Ash Wednesday - First Sunday of Lent)

Day 1 – Ash Wednesday: A Clean Heart for God

Bible Story: God Made Us

Scripture: Genesis 2:7, Psalm 51:10

A long time ago, before the mountains stood tall and before the oceans roared, God had a special plan. He was going to create something wonderful—something that would reflect His love and goodness. He had already made the sun to shine, the moon to glow, the birds to sing, and the fish to swim. But now, God wanted to create people—to be His children, to know Him, love

Him, and care for His beautiful world. So God bent down to the ground and gathered up the dust of the earth. He carefully shaped it, forming the very first person—Adam. But Adam was just a lifeless shape until something amazing happened. God leaned in and breathed His own breath into Adam's nose. Suddenly, Adam's eyes blinked open, his heart started beating, and he took his first deep breath. He was alive! God had created Adam in His own image—not just to walk and talk, but to know God, love Him, and live in friendship with Him. Later, God created Eve to be Adam's companion, and together they lived in a beautiful garden called Eden, where everything was perfect. They had pure hearts, filled with joy, peace, and love for God. But something sad happened. Sin entered the world. Adam and Eve disobeyed God, and because of that, their hearts became dirty with sin—just like ours do when we make wrong choices. Sin separates us from God. But God had a plan to make our hearts clean again.

Years later, King David understood what it meant to have a heart that needed to be cleaned.

He made mistakes too, but he prayed to God in Psalm 51:10, saying, "Create in me a clean heart, O God, and renew a right spirit within me." And that's exactly what God does! When we come to Him, say sorry for our sins, and ask for His help, He washes our hearts clean and fills them with His love!

Reflection:

Ash Wednesday is the start of Lent, a time when we prepare our hearts for Easter. The ashes we see on Ash Wednesday remind us that we need God to clean our hearts and make us new. Just like Adam was made from dust, one day our bodies will return to dust—but our souls will live forever with God if we trust in Him! Lent is a time to pray, say sorry for our sins, and grow closer to Jesus. God loves us so much that He sent Jesus to wash away our sins, giving us a fresh start!

Prayer:

Dear God, thank You for creating me and giving me life. I know that sometimes I make mistakes, but I am so thankful that You can clean my heart. Please help me to love You more each day. Amen.

Action Step:

Take a piece of paper and draw a big heart. Inside the heart, write things that can make our hearts dirty (like lying, being unkind, or disobeying). Then, take an eraser and start "erasing" those things, just like God erases our sins when we ask for forgiveness!

Day 2 – Jesus Gets Baptized: A Fresh Start

Bible Story: Jesus' Baptism

Scripture: Matthew 3:13-17

The Jordan River flowed calmly under the bright blue sky. Crowds of people had gathered along its banks, listening to a man named John the Baptist. John was a special messenger sent by God to prepare the way for Jesus. He wore clothes made of camel's hair and ate locusts and honey—a bit unusual, but John wasn't worried about fashion or fancy food. His mission was simple: call people to turn away from sin and follow God. People came from all around to listen to John's powerful message. Many felt sorry for the wrong things they had done and wanted a new beginning. So John baptized them in the river, dipping them into the water and lifting them back up—symbolizing a fresh start with God.

Then, one day, John looked up and saw Jesus walking toward him. His heart leaped with joy! He knew exactly who Jesus was—the Son of

God, the Savior of the world! But then Jesus said something surprising: "John, I want you to baptize Me." John's eyes widened. "Me? Baptize You? No, Jesus! You should be the one baptizing me!" John knew Jesus had never sinned. He was perfect! Baptism was for people who needed to be washed clean from sin—but Jesus had no sin! Jesus smiled and said, "This is the right thing to do. It is part of God's plan." John didn't argue anymore. He led Jesus into the cool waters of the Jordan River. As Jesus stood in the water, John gently lowered Him under and then lifted Him back up.

Suddenly, something amazing happened!
- The heavens opened up!
- The Holy Spirit came down from the sky like a dove and rested on Jesus!
- A powerful voice from heaven spoke, saying, "This is My beloved Son, in whom I am well pleased."

The crowd gasped in amazement. God Himself was speaking! He was announcing to the world that Jesus was His Son and that Jesus was ready to begin His mission—to teach, heal, and show people the way to God.

Reflection:

Even though Jesus was perfect, He chose to be baptized to show us the way. Baptism is a sign of a new beginning with God. It reminds us that He washes away our sins and gives us a fresh start every day! When we follow Jesus, we become God's children, and He is pleased with us too.

Prayer:

Dear Jesus, thank You for showing me how to follow You. Help me to remember that You make all things new and give me a fresh start every day. I want to live in a way that makes You happy. Amen.

Action Step:

Fill a small bowl with water. Dip your fingers in and gently touch your forehead while saying, "Jesus gives me a fresh start!" Then, thank God for loving you and helping you grow closer to Him.

Day 3 – Jesus Says No to Temptation

Bible Story: Jesus in the Wilderness

Scripture: Matthew 4:1-11

After Jesus was baptized in the Jordan River, something amazing happened—the Holy Spirit led Him into the wilderness. This was a dry, lonely place with no food, no water, and no people. Jesus stayed there for forty days and forty nights, fasting and praying. He spent time talking to God, preparing for His mission to teach the world about God's love. But while Jesus was in the wilderness, the devil came to tempt Him. The devil wanted to trick Jesus into doing wrong things instead of following God's plan. But Jesus was strong! Let's see what happened.

The First Temptation – Turning Stones into Bread

After forty days without food, Jesus was very, very hungry. His stomach growled as He walked over the hot desert sand. Just then, the devil appeared and said: "If You are the Son of God, turn these stones into bread!" Can you imagine how tempting that was? Jesus was starving, and He had the power to turn those hard rocks into warm, delicious bread. But Jesus knew that obeying God was more important than filling His stomach.

Jesus answered, "It is written: Man shall not live by bread alone, but by every word that comes from the mouth of God." (Matthew 4:4)

Jesus refused to use His power selfishly. He chose to trust God instead!

The Second Temptation – Testing God's Power Next, the devil took Jesus to the highest point of the temple in Jerusalem. Looking down, it was a long, dangerous drop to the ground. Then the devil said: "If You are the Son of God, jump down! The Bible says that God will send His angels to catch You." The devil was twisting God's words to make Jesus test God's power. But Jesus knew better. He didn't need to prove anything—He trusted God completely! So Jesus replied, "It is written: Do not put the Lord your God to the test." (Matthew 4:7) Jesus refused to test God. He trusted His Father's plan!

The Third Temptation – Worshiping the Wrong Thing

Finally, the devil took Jesus to a high mountain and showed Him all the kingdoms of the world—beautiful cities, golden palaces, and mighty armies. Then the devil said:

"I will give You all of this if You bow down and worship me." The devil wanted Jesus to take the easy way out—to have power without going to the cross. But Jesus knew that only God deserves worship! Jesus stood tall and said, "Go away, Satan! For it is written: Worship the Lord your God, and serve Him only." (Matthew 4:10)

At that moment, the devil left, and angels came to care for Jesus. He had passed every test and defeated every temptation by trusting God's Word!

Reflection:

Jesus understands what it's like to be tempted. He faced hunger, power, and pride, but He said NO to sin and YES to God. How did He do it? He used God's Word—the Bible! That's why it's important to read, learn, and remember Scripture. When we know what God says, we can stand strong against temptation, just like Jesus did!

Prayer:

Dear Jesus, thank You for showing me how to say no to sin. When I am tempted, help me to remember Your Word and choose what is right. I want to follow You with all my heart. Amen.

Action Step:

Make a "Jesus Says No" poster! On a piece of paper, write three temptations kids might face (like lying, being unkind, or disobeying). Next to each one, write a Bible verse about doing the right thing. Decorate your poster and hang it somewhere to remind you to follow Jesus' example!

Day 4 – The Calling of the Disciples

Bible Story: Jesus Chooses His Friends

Scripture: Matthew 4:18-22

The sun was beginning to set over the Sea of Galilee, turning the water into a shimmering gold. The waves gently lapped against the shore as two brothers, Simon (who was later called Peter) and Andrew, worked hard casting their fishing nets into the sea. Fishing was their job, and it wasn't easy. They would go out on their boats, throw their nets into the water, and wait—sometimes all night—hoping to catch enough fish to sell in the marketplace.

As Peter pulled up his net, a shadow fell across the boat. He looked up to see a man standing on the shore. It was Jesus! They had heard about Him before—many people were talking about this new teacher who spoke about God in a way that made hearts feel warm and full of hope. Then, Jesus spoke. "Come, follow Me, and I will make you fishers of men."

Peter and Andrew looked at each other. Fishers of men? What did that mean? But something about Jesus made them trust Him completely. Without hesitating, they dropped their nets, left their boats behind, and followed Jesus. As they walked along the shore, they saw two more brothers, James and John. They were in a boat with their father, Zebedee, fixing their nets. Jesus called to them just as He had called Peter and Andrew. James and John immediately got up, left their boat, left their father, and followed Jesus. They didn't stop to pack or to ask where they were going. They just knew they wanted to be with Jesus. One by one, Jesus called twelve disciples to follow Him—men who would walk with Him, learn from Him, and one day, share His message with the world. These men weren't kings or rich leaders. They were fishermen, tax collectors, and ordinary people. But Jesus chose them because He saw their hearts. He knew they would help change the world by sharing God's love. And just like He called them, Jesus calls us too!

Reflection:

Jesus didn't choose perfect people—He chose ordinary people, just like you and me! He doesn't look at how strong, smart, or important we are. He looks at our hearts. When we follow Jesus, we become part of His great plan to share His love with the world!

Prayer:

Dear Jesus, thank You for calling me to follow You. Help me to listen to Your voice, trust You, and love others just like You do. I want to be part of Your amazing plan! Amen.

Action Step:

Play "Follow the Leader" with your family or friends. As you play, talk about how following Jesus is the greatest adventure of all!

Day 5 (First sunday of lent) – Loving God with All Our Heart

Bible Story: The Greatest Commandment

Scripture: Matthew 22:36-40

The sun was shining over the bustling city of Jerusalem as Jesus walked through the temple courts. People gathered around Him, listening to His words. Some were amazed by His wisdom, while others—especially the religious leaders—tried to test Him. One day, a group of Pharisees, the religious teachers of the law, came up with a tricky question. One of them, a lawyer, stepped forward and asked, "Teacher, which is the greatest commandment in the Law?" The Pharisees knew that God had given many commandments in the Old Testament—613 in total! They wanted to see if Jesus would pick just one and maybe make a mistake. But Jesus knew their hearts, and He answered with words that would change everything.

Jesus said, "Love the Lord your God with all your heart, with all your soul, and with all your

mind. This is the greatest and most important commandment. And the second is like it: Love your neighbor as yourself. All the Law and the Prophets depend on these two commandments."
The people were silent for a moment. Love? They had expected a long, complicated answer. But Jesus made it simple: Love God first, and love others just like you love yourself.
Jesus' answer wasn't just about following rules it was about having a heart that truly belongs to God. When we love God with all our hearts, it changes the way we treat others. We become kind, forgiving, patient, and caring, just like Jesus!

Reflection:

Jesus taught us that love is the most important thing. We show love to God by praying, obeying Him, and trusting Him. We show love to others by being kind, sharing, forgiving, and helping. When we love God with all our hearts, it shines like a bright light for the whole world to see!

Prayer:

Dear Jesus, help me love You with all my heart, soul, and mind. Teach me to love others like You love me. I want my heart to be full of kindness and joy. Amen.

Action Step:

Make a "Love Challenge" list! Write down three ways you can love God (like praying or reading the Bible) and three ways you can love others (like helping a friend or sharing). Try to complete at least one today!

Week 2: Learning About God's Love (Second Week of Lent)

Day 6 – Zacchaeus: Jesus Loves Everyone

Bible Story: Jesus Meets Zacchaeus

Scripture: Luke 19:1-10

Jericho was a busy city. People crowded the streets, talking loudly, selling goods, and rushing to see someone very special Jesus was coming to town! Now, in Jericho, there was a man named Zacchaeus. He was a tax collector, which meant he collected money from people for the Roman government. But Zacchaeus had a big problem he often took more money than he was supposed to and kept the extra for himself. Because of this, no one liked him. People whispered about him and avoided him.

But on this special day, Zacchaeus heard that Jesus was coming. He had heard stories about Jesus how He healed the sick, made blind people see, and, most importantly, how He loved everyone, even people that others didn't like. Zacchaeus wanted to see Jesus with his own eyes. But there was a problem he was very short! No matter how hard he jumped or stretched, he couldn't see over the crowd.

Then he had an idea!

He ran ahead and climbed up a tall sycamore tree. From there, he had the perfect view! As Jesus walked closer, Zacchaeus' heart pounded with excitement. But then, something surprising happened Jesus stopped right under the tree. He looked up and called out, "Zacchaeus, come down! I'm coming to your house today!"

Zacchaeus was shocked! How did Jesus know his name? Why would Jesus want to spend time with him? Everyone else in town avoided Zacchaeus, but Jesus wanted to be his friend.

Zacchaeus climbed down quickly and happily welcomed Jesus into his home. But the crowd wasn't happy. They grumbled, "Why is Jesus spending time with a sinner like him?"

But Jesus didn't care about Zacchaeus' past. He saw Zacchaeus' heart and knew that he was ready to change. Zacchaeus stood up and said,

"Lord, I will give half of my money to the poor. And if I have cheated anyone, I will give them back four times as much!" Jesus smiled and said, "Today, salvation has come to this house. I came to find and save those who are lost." At that moment, Zacchaeus' heart was changed forever. He had found the love of Jesus—a love that forgives, heals, and welcomes everyone!

Reflection:

Zacchaeus made many mistakes, but Jesus still loved him! Jesus doesn't love us because we are perfect—He loves us because we belong to Him! No matter what we have done, Jesus welcomes us with open arms and helps us become better. Do you ever feel like no one understands you? Or like you've made mistakes? Jesus still loves you. And just like Zacchaeus, when we let Jesus into our hearts, He helps us change and follow Him!

Prayer:

Dear Jesus, thank You for loving me no matter what. I know I make mistakes, but I am so thankful that You forgive me and help me grow. Help me to love others the way You love me. Amen.

Action Step:

Climb up on a chair or a safe stepstool and pretend you are Zacchaeus in the tree. Look around and imagine seeing Jesus call your name. Now climb down and act out welcoming Jesus into your home. How would you feel? Share with your family what it means that Jesus loves everyone—even those who make mistakes!

Day 7 – Helping Friends Find Jesus

Bible Story: The Paralyzed Man is Healed

Scripture: Mark 2:1-12

There was a man who couldn't walk. He had been paralyzed for a long time, and he couldn't even get out of bed on his own. But this man had four wonderful friends who loved him so much. They knew something very important: Jesus could heal him. One day, they heard that Jesus was in town. Jesus was teaching people about God's love, and the crowd was huge—so many people came to hear Him that the house was packed, and people were standing outside, trying to listen! The paralyzed man's friends didn't give up. They wanted to help their friend meet Jesus. They thought, "We'll do whatever it takes to bring him to Jesus!" So, they carried their friend on a mat to the house. But when they got there, they saw the huge crowd. There was no way to get inside!

But the friends didn't let that stop them. They climbed up on the roof! Yes, they climbed right up, carrying their friend with them. Then, they started to dig a hole in the roof! Can you imagine how crazy this must have seemed? People were probably looking up and wondering, "What in the world is going on up there?" But the friends didn't stop. They kept digging, and finally, they made a hole big enough to lower their friend down into the room where Jesus was teaching.

Jesus saw their faith—not just the man's faith, but the faith of his friends. He smiled and said to the paralyzed man, "Son, your sins are forgiven." The people in the room were amazed! Then, Jesus said, "Get up, take your mat, and go home." And guess what? The man did exactly what Jesus said! He stood up—he was healed! He picked up his mat and walked home, praising God all the way.

Everyone in the house was amazed. They had never seen anything like it before! They said, "We have never seen anything like this!"

Reflection:

Sometimes we may have friends who are hurting or in need, just like the paralyzed man. Jesus wants us to help our friends find Him, too. Just like the friends who carried their paralyzed friend to Jesus, we can help others by showing them Jesus' love and helping them come closer to Him. We can also pray for our friends and tell them about how much Jesus loves them! If we help our friends, they might one day say, "Thank you for helping me find Jesus!"

Prayer:

Dear Jesus, thank You for my friends and family. Help me to be a good friend and to always help others find You. Show me ways I can love and help people just like You do. Amen.

Action Step:

Find a way to help a friend or family member today! Maybe you can share a kind word or help them with something they need. Afterwards, pray for them, asking Jesus to help them grow in His love. You might even want to invite them to church or to pray with you!

Day 8 – Feeding the Hungry

Bible Story: Jesus Feeds 5,000 People

Scripture: John 6:1-14

One day, Jesus was teaching and performing miracles. A huge crowd of people had gathered to listen to Him. There were 5,000 men, plus women and children! It was a huge crowd, and they had been listening to Jesus for a long time. But as the sun began to set, the people started to get hungry. They hadn't eaten anything all day, and there were no places nearby to get food. Jesus' disciples were worried. "Where are we going to find food for all these people?" they asked. But Jesus already had a plan. He asked His disciple Philip, "Where can we buy enough bread to feed all these people?"

Philip was worried, too. Even 200 silver coins wouldn't be enough to buy enough bread for all the people! Then, one of the disciples, Andrew, found a young boy who had brought his lunch. The boy had five loaves of bread and two fish. It wasn't much, but it was all he had. Jesus smiled when He saw the boy's lunch. "Bring it to me," He said. Then, He took the bread and fish, thanked God for it, and began breaking it into pieces. When He gave the bread and fish to His disciples, something amazing happened. The food never ran out! They passed the bread and fish to everyone in the crowd. All 5,000 people ate and were full! And there were even 12 baskets of leftovers! The people were amazed. They realized that Jesus wasn't just an ordinary teacher—He had the power to do miracles. The boy had given Jesus a small lunch, and Jesus had turned it into enough food to feed a huge crowd.

Reflection:

Jesus showed us that God cares about our needs. Even though the people were hungry, Jesus didn't ignore them. He provided for them in a way that was way beyond what anyone expected. When we feel like we don't have enough or can't do enough, we can trust that God can take what we have and use it to do amazing things. Just like Jesus fed the people, He also wants to feed our hearts with His love and kindness. When we share what we have with others, Jesus can do amazing things through us.

Prayer:

Dear Jesus, thank You for caring about my needs and for always providing for me. Help me to share what I have with others, just like You shared with the crowd. Thank You for Your love and the way You care for everyone. Amen.

Action Step:

Today, think about something you can share with others. It might be something as simple as a snack, your time, or even a smile! Take a moment to pray and ask Jesus how He wants you to help and care for others, just like He did.

Day 9 – Loving Our Enemies

Bible Story: Jesus Teaches About Love

Scripture: Matthew 5:43-48

One day, Jesus was teaching the people about how to love others. He said something that was very surprising. He told them, "You have heard that you should love your neighbors and hate your enemies. But I tell you, love your enemies. Pray for those who hurt you."

Now, this was a very hard thing for the people to understand. They thought that if someone was mean to them or their friends, they didn't have to be nice to that person. They wanted to treat their enemies just like their enemies treated them. But Jesus said that loving your enemies is one of the most important things you can do. Jesus explained, "If you love only those who love you, what's so special about that? Even bad people love people who are nice to them. But if you love your enemies, if you pray for those who hurt you, you will show that you are different. You will show that you are my followers." He also told them, "God loves everyone, even those who don't love Him back. If you want to be like God, you need to love everyone, even the people who aren't kind to you."

This was a big challenge. It was hard to love people who were mean to you. But Jesus said that when we love our enemies, we show God's love to the world. And when we pray for others, even those who hurt us, we become more like Jesus.

Reflection:

Loving our enemies sounds really hard, doesn't it? Sometimes people are mean to us or hurt our feelings, and it's so easy to want to get back at them or ignore them. But Jesus wants us to show love and kindness to everyone, even when it's hard. When we pray for others, even people who are unkind, we are showing that we trust Jesus to help us be more loving and more like Him. Remember, Jesus didn't just love the people who were kind to Him—He loved everyone, even those who didn't love Him back. We can be like Jesus by loving all people, even when it's hard.

Prayer:

Dear Jesus, thank You for loving me even when I make mistakes. Help me to love others, especially when they are unkind to me. Teach me to forgive and show kindness, just like You do. Amen.

Action Step:

Think of someone who might not be very kind to you or someone who has hurt your feelings. Pray for them today, asking Jesus to help you love them with a kind heart. Maybe you can also do something kind for that person, even if they don't deserve it. Jesus loves us even when we don't deserve it, and we can share that love with others!

Day 10 – A Thankful Heart

Bible Story: The Grateful Leper

Scripture: Luke 17:11-19

One day, as Jesus was traveling, He came across a group of ten men who were suffering from a terrible disease called leprosy. Leprosy made their skin look very sick and was contagious, so the men had to live away from everyone else. They couldn't hug their families or friends, and they were very lonely.

When the ten men saw Jesus, they called out, "Jesus, Master, have pity on us!" They had heard that Jesus could heal people, and they were desperate for His help. Jesus looked at them and said, "Go, show yourselves to the priests." You see, back in those days, if a person thought they were healed from leprosy, they had to go to a priest to be checked and declared clean. So, the men obeyed Jesus and started walking to the priest. As they walked, something amazing happened. They were healed! Their sick skin became healthy, and they were no longer suffering from leprosy! But here's where the story gets interesting. Out of the ten men, only one of them turned back to Jesus. This man was so thankful for the healing that he ran back to Jesus, praising God and shouting, "Thank You, Jesus!" He fell down at Jesus' feet and thanked Him for making him well. Jesus asked, "Were not all ten healed? Where are the other nine? Has no one returned to give praise to God except this foreigner?" And then, Jesus said to the man, "Rise and go; your faith has made you well."

Reflection:

The one man who came back to say thank you is a great example for us. Jesus healed ten people, but only one person was truly grateful enough to come back and thank Him. Being thankful to God is an important part of our relationship with Him. When we remember to say thank you for the good things God does for us—big and small—we show Him that we appreciate His love and care. We don't want to be like the other nine men who forgot to say thank you. Let's make sure we remember to be thankful, just like the man who came back to Jesus. We can thank

God for our family, our friends, our health, and everything good in our lives. A thankful heart helps us grow closer to God and see His goodness in our lives.

Prayer:

Dear Jesus, thank You for all the wonderful things You have given me. Thank You for my family, my friends, and the things I enjoy. Help me to always remember to say thank You for all Your blessings. I am so grateful for Your love. Amen.

Action Step:

Today, take a moment to thank God for something special in your life. You can write it down in a journal, say it out loud in prayer, or share it with your family. Maybe even take a thank-you card and write a note to someone who has blessed you, just to show them you appreciate them! A thankful heart makes us feel closer to God and others.

Day 11 – The Prodigal Son Returns Home

Bible Story: A Father's Unfailing Love

Scripture: Luke 15:11-32

There was a father who had two sons. One day, the younger son said to his father, "Father, give me my share of the inheritance now." Normally, children would get their inheritance after their parents died, but this son wanted it right away. The father was sad, but he gave his son what he asked for. The younger son then left home and traveled to a faraway place. He spent all his money on things that didn't make him happy. He bought food, clothes, and even threw big parties. But soon, he ran out of money. Without any money left, the son had to find work. He got a job feeding pigs, and he was so hungry that he even thought about eating the food the pigs were eating! Finally, the young man realized how foolish he had been. He said to himself, "I will go back to my father. He treats his workers better than this. I will ask him to forgive me." So, the son started his journey back home. As he was still a long way off, his father saw him coming and ran to him with open arms. The father was so happy to see his son again that he hugged him and kissed him. The son said, "Father, I have sinned against heaven and against you. I am no longer worthy to be called your son." But the father didn't care about that. He said, "Quick! Bring the best robe and put it on him! Put a ring on his finger and sandals on his feet. Let's celebrate, for my son was lost and is now found!" The father threw a big party to celebrate the return of his son. But the older son, who had stayed home and worked hard, was not happy. He was upset that his father was throwing a party for the younger son who had been so careless with his money. But the father said, "You are always with me, and everything I have is yours. But we had to celebrate because your brother was lost and is now found."

Reflection:

This story, called the Parable of the Prodigal Son, teaches us about God's love for us. The father in the story is like God, and the son is like us. Even when we make bad choices and wander away from God, God is always ready to forgive us and welcome us back with open arms. The son felt ashamed and unworthy when he returned, but his father didn't care about that. He was just happy to have his son back. This shows us that no matter how far we may wander away from God, He is always waiting for us to come back to Him. When we say sorry to God and ask for His forgiveness, He is always ready to forgive us, no matter what we've done. God's love is so big and kind that He will always welcome us back into His arms.

Prayer:

Dear God, thank You for always welcoming me back when I make mistakes. Help me to remember that You love me no matter what and that I can always come to You for forgiveness. Thank You for Your kindness and mercy. Amen.

Action Step:

Today, think about any mistakes or things you've done that you want to ask God to forgive you for. Talk to God about it and say you're sorry. Remember that He will always forgive you and welcome you back, just like the father in the story. You can also forgive others who may have hurt you, just like God forgives us.

Day 12 (second sunday of lent) – God's Love Never Fails

Bible Story: Nothing Can Separate Us from God's Love

Scripture: Romans 8:38-39

In the book of Romans, the apostle Paul tells us about something wonderful. He says that nothing—not even the worst things we can think of—can ever separate us from God's love. Let's look at what Paul wrote: "For I am convinced that neither death nor life, neither angels nor demons, neither the present nor the future, nor any powers, neither height nor depth, nor anything else in all creation, will be able to separate us from the love of God that is in Christ Jesus our Lord." That's a huge promise! Paul is saying that no matter what happens in our lives, God will always love us. Whether we are happy, sad, or scared, whether things are going well or if we're going through a tough time—God's love is always with us. Think about all the things that could make you feel lonely or scared. Maybe you're worried about something happening at school, or maybe you miss someone you love. God's love is bigger than all of that. No matter how hard life may seem, God promises that His love will never leave us. Just like a parent's love for their child doesn't end, God's love for us is unchanging and strong. No matter where we go or what we do, His love will always be there to comfort us, protect us, and guide us. God's love never fails.

Reflection:

Sometimes life gets tough, and we might feel like things are out of control. We might wonder if anyone cares or if we are loved. But the truth is, God loves us deeply. His love is never-ending. There's nothing that can take it away from us—no problem too big, no fear too strong, no mistake too bad. When we are feeling sad or afraid, we can remember that God's love is always with us. He will never leave us, and we can always talk to Him. Even when we don't see Him, His love is right there beside us, holding us close.

Prayer:

Dear God, thank You for loving me with a love that never ends. Help me to remember that no matter what happens, Your love will always be with me. Thank You for never leaving me, even when things feel hard or scary. I trust that Your love will always be there to guide and protect me. Amen.

Action Step:

Today, think about a time when you felt loved by God. Maybe it was when you were with your family, when you were praying, or even just when you felt peace in your heart. Take a moment to thank God for His unfailing love. You can also share this amazing truth with someone else! Maybe tell a friend or family member, "God's love never fails!"

Week 3: Jesus Teaches Us About God's Kingdom (Third Week of Lent)

Day 13 – The Beatitudes: Blessings from Jesus

Bible Story: Jesus Teaches on the Mountain

Scripture: Matthew 5:1-12

One day, Jesus went up to a mountain with His disciples. When He saw the large crowd of people following Him, He sat down and began to teach them about God's kingdom. What He said was very special. He taught them what it means to be blessed by God, and the things that would make them happy and bring them peace. These teachings are called the Beatitudes, which means "blessings."

Jesus told them:

- "Blessed are the poor in spirit, for theirs is the kingdom of heaven."

- "Blessed are those who mourn, for they will be comforted."
- "Blessed are the meek, for they will inherit the earth."
- "Blessed are those who hunger and thirst for righteousness, for they will be filled."
- "Blessed are the merciful, for they will be shown mercy."
- "Blessed are the pure in heart, for they will see God."
- "Blessed are the peacemakers, for they will be called children of God."
- "Blessed are those who are persecuted because of righteousness, for theirs is the kingdom of heaven." Jesus was telling everyone that God's kingdom is different from what we might expect. In His kingdom, humility, kindness, mercy, and love are the most important things. People who may not seem strong in the world, like those who are sad, poor in spirit, or gentle, are the ones who are truly blessed. When we live in a way that reflects these teachings, we show others that we are following Jesus and living for Him. Even if the world doesn't always

understand or honor us, Jesus promises that we are blessed by God and that we will be comforted and rewarded.

Reflection:

The Beatitudes show us how to live as citizens of God's kingdom. They teach us to be humble, loving, kind, and forgiving. Sometimes, the world may tell us that we need to be the best or the strongest, but Jesus teaches us that true blessing comes from being kind, merciful, and peaceful. When we care for others and show love, we are showing God's kingdom in action. Jesus wants us to remember that even if we are going through difficult times, He sees us and He blesses us. God's kingdom is not about what we have or how powerful we are; it's about how we love and serve others.

Prayer:

Dear Jesus, thank You for teaching us about Your kingdom. Help me to be humble and kind, to show mercy, and to be a peacemaker in my life. Please help me to always remember that being a blessing to others is how I show Your love. Amen.

Action Step:
Today, think about one of the Beatitudes and find a way to live it out. Maybe you can show kindness to someone who needs help or forgive someone who has hurt you. You can also be a peacemaker by helping solve a disagreement between friends. Remember, even small acts of love and kindness can show God's kingdom to the world!

Day 14 – Be a Light for Jesus

Bible Story: A Lamp on a Stand

Scripture: Matthew 5:14-16

One day, while Jesus was teaching a crowd of people, He spoke about light. He said, "You are the light of the world. A town built on a hill cannot be hidden." What did He mean by that? Think about it! If you're up on a tall hill, everyone can see you from far away, right? You can't hide a city that's high up, and Jesus was telling His followers that they are like that city on the hill—they should be shining God's light for everyone to see. Then, Jesus told them something very important: "Neither do people light a lamp and put it under a bowl. Instead, they put it on its stand, and it gives light to everyone in the house." Imagine if you turned on a lamp and then covered it up with a bowl. What would happen? It would be dark, right? The light wouldn't be able to shine! That's what Jesus was trying to say: Don't hide your light. If you know God's love, if you are filled with His light, you shouldn't keep it hidden. You should let it shine out for the world to see! Then Jesus said, "In the same way, let your light shine before others, that they may see your good deeds and glorify your Father in heaven." Jesus was telling His followers that when they let their light shine by doing good deeds, others would see those deeds and praise God. Just like a lamp brightens a room, our good actions can help brighten the world and show others how good and loving God is.

Reflection:

Jesus calls us to be lights in the world. We don't have to be perfect to shine God's light, but we do have to let our good deeds and our love for others show. When we act with kindness, honesty, and love, we are shining the light of Jesus. Our lives should be like lamps, shining brightly so that others can see God's goodness. Think about how light works. A light shines for everyone. It doesn't pick and choose who it will shine on. God wants us to love everyone, just like Jesus did. When we let our light shine through good deeds, it can help others know more about God's love. Whether we're helping a friend, showing kindness to a neighbor, or simply sharing a smile, our actions can bring God's light to people around us.

Prayer:

Dear Jesus, thank You for being the Light of the world. Please help me to shine Your light in everything I do. Show me how I can love others and be kind to everyone I meet. Help my actions to reflect Your love so that others can see how amazing You are. Amen.

Action Step:

Today, think of one way you can let your light shine for others. Maybe you can help a friend who is having a hard time, share something with someone in need, or even just say something kind to a classmate. Remember, small acts of kindness are like little lights shining in a dark room. You can also talk to your family about ways to be a light together, like doing a good deed as a group or helping someone outside your home.

Day 15 – The Good Samaritan: Loving Others

Bible Story: Helping Those in Need

Scripture: Luke 10:25-37

One day, a teacher of the law stood up to test Jesus. He asked, "Teacher, what must I do to inherit eternal life?" Jesus replied by asking him what the Scriptures said. The teacher answered, "Love the Lord your God with all your heart, soul, strength, and mind, and love your neighbor as yourself." "You have answered correctly," Jesus replied. "Do this, and you will live." But the teacher wanted to be sure he understood, so he asked, "Who is my neighbor?" To answer this question, Jesus told a story. He said: There was once a man traveling from Jerusalem to Jericho, a very dangerous road. On the way, he was attacked by robbers. They beat him, took his clothes, and left him lying half-dead on the road. Soon, a priest came down the road. When he saw the man, he passed by on the other side, not stopping to help. Then a Levite, a man who worked in the temple, came along. He too saw the man, but he passed by on the other side without helping. But then, a Samaritan, someone from a group who was not liked by the Jewish people, came walking by. When he saw the hurt man, he felt compassion for him. The Samaritan went over, bandaged his wounds, and took him to an inn to take care of him. The Samaritan even paid for the man's stay and promised to help with anything else the man needed. Jesus asked the teacher, "Which of these three do you think was a neighbor to the man who fell into the hands of robbers?" The teacher replied, "The one who had mercy on him."

Jesus said, "Go and do likewise."

Reflection:

In this story, Jesus teaches us that a true neighbor is anyone who needs our help, no matter who they are or where they come from. The priest and the Levite walked by the hurt man, but the Samaritan stopped to help, even though he wasn't expected to. Jesus shows us that love means helping those in need, even if they're different from us. We are called to love everyone, and this means being kind and helping those who may need it the most. Sometimes, loving others means stepping out of our comfort zone, like the Samaritan did, and showing kindness even when it's not easy. Jesus wants us to help, love, and show mercy to everyone, not just the people we know or those who are like us. Loving others means treating them with care, just like Jesus would.

Prayer:

Dear Jesus, thank You for teaching me how to love others. Please help me to be kind to everyone, even those who might be different from me. Show me when I can help someone in need, and give me a loving heart like the Good Samaritan. Amen.

Action Step:

Think of one way you can show love and kindness to someone who may need help today. Maybe you can help a classmate with their schoolwork, assist a family member with something around the house, or lend a hand to someone who is having a hard time. Remember, even small acts of kindness show the love of Jesus to others. You could also share the story of the Good Samaritan with a friend or family member to encourage them to love and help others too!

Day 16 – The Mustard Seed: Growing in Faith

Bible Story: Faith Like a Tiny Seed

Scripture: Matthew 13:31-32

One day, as Jesus was teaching a large crowd, He wanted to help them understand how God's kingdom works. The people gathered around, eager to hear what Jesus had to say. He loved using parables—stories with special meanings—to explain important truths. Jesus said, "The kingdom of heaven is like a mustard seed, which a man took and planted in his field." The people in the crowd knew exactly what a mustard seed looked like. It was one of the tiniest seeds you could find! If you held it in your hand, it would be barely bigger than a speck of dust. Some people might think that such a small seed couldn't do anything special. But Jesus had more to say. "Though it is the smallest of all seeds, yet when it grows, it is the largest of garden plants and becomes a tree, so that the birds come and perch in its branches."

Imagine a tiny mustard seed being planted in the ground. At first, you can hardly see it. But with water, sunlight, and time, the seed starts to grow. First, a small green sprout pops up from the soil. Then, little by little, it stretches taller and taller until it becomes a huge tree, big enough for birds to rest in its branches! The people listening to Jesus must have been amazed. How could something so tiny grow into something so big and strong? Jesus was showing them (and us!) that even a little faith can grow into something amazing. When we trust God, our faith might start small, but over time, it grows stronger and stronger—just like the mustard seed grows into a big tree.

Reflection:

Have you ever planted a seed before? At first, it looks like nothing is happening. But under the soil, something wonderful is taking place. The seed is beginning to grow! Faith is just like that. Maybe you feel like your faith is small, like a tiny mustard seed. Maybe you wonder, "Can God really use me? Can I really make a difference?" Jesus wants you to know that even a small amount of faith is powerful. When you believe in Him and trust Him, your faith grows stronger every day.

Just like a tree provides shade and a home for birds, your faith can bless others. When you show kindness, love, and trust in God, people around you will notice. They might even want to learn more about Jesus because of you!

Prayer:

Dear Jesus, thank You for showing me that my faith can grow, just like a tiny mustard seed becomes a big tree. Sometimes my faith feels small, but I know You can make it strong. Please help me to trust You more and believe that You can do great things in my life. Amen.

Action Step:

Today, find a small seed and plant it in a cup of soil or your backyard. Water it and watch it grow over time. Every time you see it, remember that your faith is growing too! If you don't have a seed, draw a big tree and write "Faith" on it. Then, add small leaves or branches each time you pray, read the Bible, or show kindness—things that help your faith grow!

Day 17 – Building Our Lives on Jesus

Bible Story: The Wise and Foolish Builders

Scripture: Matthew 7:24-27

One day, Jesus was teaching His followers about how to live in a way that honors God. He wanted them to understand that hearing His words is important, but actually obeying them is even more important. So, He told them a story about two men who built houses—but in very different ways. Jesus said, "Everyone who hears My words and puts them into practice is like a wise man who built his house on the rock." The wise builder chose a strong, solid rock as the foundation for his house. He carefully built it so that it would stand tall and firm. One day, a big storm came—the rain poured, the wind howled, and the waters rose. But the house did not fall because it was built on a strong foundation! Then Jesus said, "But everyone who hears My words and does not put them into practice is like a foolish man who built his house on the sand." The foolish builder wanted to build his house quickly, so he picked soft, shaky sand as his foundation. It looked fine at first, but then the same storm came—the rain poured, the wind howled, and the waters rose. But this time, the house came crashing down! The sand wasn't strong enough to hold it up.

Jesus finished by saying, "Great was its fall!" The people listening to Him understood that He wasn't just talking about houses—He was teaching them about how to live their lives.

Reflection:

Imagine building a sandcastle at the beach. It looks beautiful, but when the waves come, it washes away. Now, think about a strong house made of bricks and built on a rock. No matter how hard the wind blows, it stays standing!

Jesus wants us to build our lives on Him, just like the wise builder built his house on the rock. That means we don't just listen to Jesus' words—we obey them and live by them.

- When we love others like Jesus taught us, we are building on the rock.

- When we pray and trust God, we are building on the rock.
- When we choose what is right instead of what is easy, we are building on the rock.

But if we ignore Jesus' teachings, it's like building on sand—when hard times come, our faith won't be strong enough to stand.

Let's be wise builders and make Jesus the foundation of our lives!

Prayer:

Dear Jesus, I want to be like the wise builder. Help me to listen to Your words and obey them. I don't want my life to be built on things that won't last. Please make my faith strong so that when hard times come, I will stand firm in You. Amen.

Action Step:

Find two small objects (like toy houses or blocks). Fill a tray with sand and put one object on it. Then, take a solid rock and place the other object on top. Now, gently shake the tray or pour a little water over it. What happens? The object on the sand falls, but the one on the rock stays firm! Remember—when we build our lives on

Jesus, we can stand strong no matter what comes!

Day 18 – Trusting Jesus in the Storm

Bible Story: Jesus Calms the Storm

Scripture: Mark 4:35-41

One evening, after a long day of teaching and helping people, Jesus told His disciples, "Let's go to the other side of the lake." So, they got into a boat and started sailing across the water.

At first, everything was calm. The waves gently rocked the boat, and the stars began to twinkle in the sky. Jesus, feeling tired from the day, lay down at the back of the boat and fell asleep. But then, something scary happened. A huge storm suddenly appeared! The wind roared, the waves grew bigger, and water started splashing into the boat. The disciples were terrified.

They tried to row harder, but the storm was too strong. The boat rocked wildly, and they thought they were going to sink! In their fear, they ran to

Jesus, who was still sleeping peacefully. "Jesus! Wake up! Don't you care that we're about to drown?" they shouted. Jesus opened His eyes, stood up, and looked at the storm. Then, in a calm and powerful voice, He said, "Peace, be still!" At that very moment, the wind stopped howling, the waves became calm, and the storm disappeared completely. The sea was as smooth as glass. Jesus turned to His disciples and asked, "Why are you so afraid? Do you still not have faith?" The disciples were amazed. They looked at each other and said, "Who is this? Even the wind and the waves obey Him!" They had seen Jesus heal people, teach amazing lessons, and do many miracles, but this was incredible. Even the storm listened to Jesus!

Reflection:

Have you ever felt afraid? Maybe a thunderstorm outside made you nervous, or you were scared about something at school. Just like the disciples, we all have storms in our lives—times when we feel worried, afraid, or unsure. But this story reminds us that Jesus is always with us. Even when life feels stormy,

Jesus is in our boat. He is powerful enough to calm the wind and the waves, and He is powerful enough to bring us peace when we are scared.

Sometimes, Jesus calms the storm around us, like He did on the lake. Other times, He calms our hearts, helping us to trust Him even when things don't change right away. Either way, we can trust Jesus completely. When we feel afraid, we can pray and remember that Jesus is always in control. He loves us, and He will never let us face the storm alone.

Prayer:

Dear Jesus, sometimes I feel afraid, just like the disciples did. But I know that You are always with me. Help me to trust You, even when things feel scary. Thank You for loving me and giving me peace. Amen.

Action Step:

Fill a bowl with water and gently blow on it to make little waves. Imagine the disciples feeling afraid in their boat. Then, say, "Peace, be still!" and stop blowing. Watch how the water calms down. Just like that, Jesus can calm our hearts when we feel afraid. The next time you feel worried, take a deep breath and remember: Jesus is in your boat!

Day 19 – God Cares for Us

Bible Story: Do Not Worry, God Provides

Scripture: Matthew 6:25-34

One day, Jesus sat on a hillside with a large group of people gathered around Him. He knew that many of them worried about their daily needs—what they would eat, what they would wear, and how they would take care of their families. So, He began to teach them about trusting God. Jesus said, "Do not worry about your life—what you will eat or drink, or about your body and what you will wear. Isn't life more than food and clothing?" Then, He pointed to the birds flying in the sky. "Look at the birds," Jesus said. "They don't plant seeds or store food in barns, but God feeds them. And aren't you much more valuable than birds?" The people nodded. Birds didn't worry about their next meal—God always provided for them! Then, Jesus pointed to the beautiful flowers in the field. "Look at the lilies," He said. "They don't work or make clothes, but even King

Solomon—who was the richest king—was never dressed as beautifully as these flowers. If God cares so much about the flowers, which are here today and gone tomorrow, won't He care even more about you?" The crowd listened closely. Jesus wasn't saying that food and clothes weren't important. He was saying that God already knows what we need and will take care of us. Jesus told them, "Instead of worrying, seek God's kingdom first, and everything you need will be given to you." Then, He finished by saying, "Do not worry about tomorrow. Let tomorrow take care of itself." The people left that day with peace in their hearts, knowing that God loved them and would always take care of them.

Reflection:

Do you ever worry about things? Maybe you wonder if you'll have enough time to finish your homework, if your parents will always take care of you, or if something bad might happen. Jesus tells us not to worry because God is always in control. He takes care of the birds and the flowers, and He loves you even more! That means He will always provide what you need. Worrying doesn't change anything, but trusting God gives us peace. Instead of being afraid, we can pray, believe, and rest in God's love. So the next time you feel worried, remember the birds and the flowers—if God takes care of them, He will surely take care of you!

Prayer:

Dear God, sometimes I feel worried about things in my life. But I know You love me and will always take care of me. Help me to trust You instead of being afraid. Thank You for always providing for me. Amen.

Action Step:

Go outside and look for birds or flowers. Watch how birds fly freely and how flowers bloom beautifully. They don't worry—God takes care of them. Every time you see a bird or a flower this week, remember that God is taking care of you too!

Week 4: Walking with Jesus to the Cross (Fourth Week of Lent)

Day 20 – Palm Sunday: Jesus Enters Jerusalem

Bible Story: The Triumphal Entry

Scripture: Matthew 21:1-11

It was time for the Passover festival, a special time when people traveled to Jerusalem to celebrate and worship God. The city was full of excitement, and crowds of people were gathering to see Jesus. As Jesus and His disciples approached Jerusalem, He gave two of them a special task.

"Go to the next village," Jesus said. "There you will find a donkey and her colt. Untie them and bring them to Me. If anyone asks why, just say, 'The Lord needs them.'" The disciples obeyed and found everything exactly as Jesus had said. They brought the donkey and its young colt to

Jesus. The disciples placed their cloaks on the donkey's back, and Jesus sat on it, riding toward Jerusalem. As Jesus entered the city, a large crowd gathered. People were so excited to see Him! They began to lay their cloaks on the road, while others cut palm branches from the trees and spread them on the ground.

The people waved their palm branches and shouted, "Hosanna! Hosanna to the Son of David! Blessed is He who comes in the name of the Lord!" They knew Jesus was special, and they welcomed Him like a king. They had heard about His miracles, His kindness, and His teachings. Many believed He was the promised Savior, But not everyone was happy. Some of the religious leaders didn't like the attention Jesus was getting. They told Him, "Tell these people to be quiet!" But Jesus replied, "If they keep quiet, even the stones will cry out!"

Jesus rode humbly into Jerusalem, not on a war horse like an earthly king, but on a gentle donkey—a sign that He came in peace and love.

Reflection:

Imagine being in that crowd—waving a palm branch, shouting "Hosanna," and celebrating Jesus as He entered the city. It must have been so exciting! But just a few days later, some of the same people would turn away from Jesus. They expected Him to be a king who would fight for them, but Jesus came to give His life for them instead. Jesus is still our King today—not a king with a golden crown and a big palace, but a King who rules with love, kindness, and peace. He came to rescue us from sin and give us eternal life. We don't need palm branches to celebrate Jesus. We can praise Him by singing, praying, and telling others about His love every day!

Prayer:
Dear Jesus, You are my King! Thank You for coming to save us and showing us how to love. Help me to praise You not just with my words but with my actions. Hosanna! I celebrate You today and always. Amen.

Action Step:
Make your own palm branch! Take a piece of green paper and cut out the shape of a palm leaf. If you don't have green paper, you can color a

white sheet. Write the word "Hosanna" on it and wave it while saying, "Jesus is my King!" You can even sing a song to praise Him!

Day 21 – Jesus Cleans the Temple

Bible Story: Jesus Teaches About True Worship

Scripture: Mark 11:15-17

The day after Jesus entered Jerusalem, He went to the Temple, the special place where people came to pray and worship God. But when He got there, He saw something that made Him very upset. Instead of people praying and worshiping, the Temple was filled with moneychangers and merchants selling animals for sacrifices. People were buying and selling, shouting about prices, and treating God's house like a marketplace instead of a place of prayer.

Jesus was filled with righteous anger. He knew the Temple was meant to be a holy place, not a place for greed and dishonesty.

So, Jesus did something bold. He began to turn over the tables of the moneychangers and the merchants, sending their coins rolling across the floor. He set the cages open, letting the birds fly free. The people were shocked! Then, Jesus said loudly, "The Scriptures say, 'My house will be called a house of prayer for all nations,' but you have turned it into a den of thieves!" The religious leaders were angry. They didn't like how Jesus challenged them. But the people, especially the children, were amazed. They saw that Jesus cared about God's house and wanted everyone to worship God with honest and pure hearts.

That day, Jesus showed that worship is about loving God, not about money or selfishness.

Reflection:

Jesus was passionate about true worship. He didn't want people using the Temple to make money—He wanted them to honor God.

Today, we don't worship God in the same kind of Temple, but our hearts are like temples for God. Jesus wants our hearts to be clean and full of love for Him. Do you ever let things get in the way of worshiping God? Maybe you're distracted when you pray, or maybe you focus too much on other things instead of spending time with God.

Let's ask Jesus to clean our hearts just like He cleaned the Temple, so we can worship Him with joy and honesty.

Prayer:

Dear Jesus, thank You for teaching us how to worship You the right way. Please help me keep my heart clean, focused on You, and full of love. I want to worship You with all my heart. Amen.

Action Step:

Take five minutes today to clean your room or tidy up a space in your house. As you clean, remember how Jesus cleaned the Temple. When your room is neat, sit down and pray. Ask Jesus to help keep your heart clean so you can worship Him with love!

Day 22 – The Last Supper: Jesus' Special Meal

Bible Story: Jesus Shares Bread and Wine

Scripture: Luke 22:14-20

It was the night before Jesus would go to the cross. He gathered with His twelve disciples in an upstairs room to eat a special meal together. This meal was part of the Passover, a time when God's people remembered how He saved them long ago. Jesus knew this would be His last supper with His disciples before He went to die for the sins of the world. The disciples didn't fully understand what was about to happen, but Jesus wanted to prepare them for what was coming. As they sat at the table, Jesus picked up a loaf of bread. He held it in His hands, gave thanks to God, and then broke the bread into pieces. He passed it to His disciples and said,
"This is My body, given for you. Do this in remembrance of Me." Then, He took a cup of wine, gave thanks, and passed it around the table. He told them,

"This cup is the new covenant in My blood, poured out for you." Jesus was telling them that He was about to give His life for them, just like the Passover lamb that was sacrificed to save God's people long ago. His body would be broken, and His blood would be poured out, but it would bring forgiveness and new life to all who believed in Him. After supper, Jesus looked at His disciples with love and sadness. He knew one of them, Judas, would soon betray Him, but He still chose to show love to everyone at the table. Then, they sang a hymn and went out to the Garden of Gethsemane, where Jesus would pray. That night, Jesus showed His disciples the greatest act of love—He was willing to die for them and for all of us.

Reflection:

Imagine sitting at that table with Jesus. How would you feel if He handed you the bread and the cup, telling you it was His body and blood given for you? Jesus gave us the Lord's Supper (Communion) so we would always remember His great love and sacrifice. Every time we take the bread and the cup, we are remembering how much Jesus loves us and how He died to save us. Jesus wants us to thank Him, trust Him, and live for Him every day.

Prayer:

Dear Jesus, thank You for loving me so much that You gave Your life for me. Help me to always remember Your great love and to live in a way that honors You. Amen.

Action Step:

With your family, share a special meal together. Before eating, take a moment to thank Jesus for His love and sacrifice. You can break a piece of bread and say, "Jesus gave His life for us." If you want, you can also sing a simple worship song together, just like Jesus and His disciples did!

Day 23 – Jesus Washes His Disciples' Feet

Bible Story: A Lesson in Serving Others

Scripture: John 13:3-17

It was the night of the Last Supper, and Jesus and His disciples had gathered in an upstairs room. The meal was ready, but something was missing. In those days, people walked everywhere on dusty roads in sandals. Their feet would get very dirty. Usually, a servant would wash the guests' feet before dinner, but this time, no one had done it. The disciples sat down, waiting for someone else to do the job. No one wanted to be the one to wash dirty feet—that was a servant's job!
But then, something surprising happened. Jesus, their Teacher and Lord, stood up from the table. He took off His robe, wrapped a towel around His waist, and poured water into a basin. One by one, He knelt down and began washing the disciples' feet! The room fell silent. Why was Jesus, the Son of God, doing this? When Jesus came to Peter, Peter shook his head. "Lord, are

You going to wash my feet?" Peter asked. "No, You will never wash my feet!" But Jesus looked at Peter with love and said, "If I don't wash you, you won't belong to Me." Peter gasped. "Then, Lord, wash all of me—my hands, my head, everything!"

Jesus smiled and said, "You are already clean. But I am doing this to show you how to serve one another." After Jesus had washed everyone's feet, He stood up and said, "Do you understand what I have done for you? You call Me 'Teacher' and 'Lord,' and that is true. But if I, your Lord and Teacher, have washed your feet, you should wash each other's feet. I have given you an example. Now go and do the same." Jesus was showing them something very important—in God's Kingdom, the greatest person is the one who serves others.

Reflection:

Can you imagine how surprised the disciples were when Jesus, the Son of God, washed their feet? Jesus showed them that true love means serving others. Sometimes, we want to be the greatest—to be first, to be the leader, to be in charge. But Jesus teaches us that the greatest person is the one who helps others. How can you serve others today? Maybe by helping a friend, sharing with a sibling, or being kind to someone who is sad. When we serve others with love, we are following Jesus' example.

Prayer:

Dear Jesus, thank You for showing us what it means to serve. Help me to have a heart like Yours, always willing to help others with love and kindness. Amen.

Action Step:

Do something kind for someone today! You can help a family member, share with a friend, or clean up without being asked.

If you want, you can even wash someone's feet at home, just like Jesus did! Fill a small bowl with warm water, grab a towel, and gently wash a family member's feet to show love and kindness.

Day 24 – Jesus Prays in the Garden

Bible Story: Jesus in Gethsemane

Scripture: Matthew 26:36-46

It was a quiet night, and the moonlight gently shone down on the garden of Gethsemane. After eating the Last Supper with His disciples, Jesus led them to this peaceful garden to pray. Jesus knew that trouble was coming. He had already told His friends that He would soon be taken away, and He was feeling heavy-hearted about what was about to happen. Jesus turned to Peter, James, and John, three of His closest friends, and said, "My heart is very sad. I feel so burdened with the weight of what's about to happen. Stay here with Me and keep watch while I go and pray."

As Jesus walked alone into the garden, He began to pray to His Father. He fell to the ground, overwhelmed with the pain of knowing that He would soon suffer for the sins of the world. Jesus prayed, "Father, if it is possible, take this cup of suffering away from Me. But I want Your will to be done, not Mine." Jesus knew the path ahead would be filled with pain and sorrow, but He trusted God's plan. He wasn't just praying for Himself, but also for the world—because He knew that He was the only one who could save everyone from sin. After praying, Jesus went back to His disciples, hoping they had been awake and praying with Him. But when He found them, they had fallen asleep! "Couldn't you stay awake and pray with Me for one hour?" Jesus asked them gently. "Watch and pray so that you will not fall into temptation. The spirit is willing, but the flesh is weak." Then Jesus went away a second time and prayed again, saying, "Father, if this cup cannot be taken away unless I drink it, may Your will be done."

After praying, Jesus returned to find His disciples asleep once more. They couldn't stay awake to keep watch with Him. Jesus left them again, praying a third time, with the same words. His heart was heavy, but He was determined to do what God had called Him to do. Finally, Jesus came back and said to His disciples, "Are you still sleeping and resting? Look, the time has come. The Son of Man is about to be betrayed into the hands of sinners. Rise, let us go. Here comes My betrayer." As Jesus finished speaking, He saw Judas, one of His own disciples, coming toward Him with a crowd of soldiers and guards. Judas had betrayed Jesus for thirty silver coins and would greet Him with a kiss to signal that He was the one they should arrest.

Reflection:

Have you ever felt so worried or sad that you didn't know what to do? Jesus felt the same way that night. He knew He was going to face great suffering, and His heart was full of fear and sadness. But instead of hiding or running away, Jesus chose to pray. He talked to His Father and asked for strength. He trusted that God's plan was the best, even though it was very hard for Him. When you feel afraid or sad, you can also talk to God. He will listen, and He will give you the strength you need. You can trust that He is always with you, just as He was with Jesus in the garden.

Prayer:

Dear Jesus, thank You for showing me how to pray when I feel scared or sad. Help me to trust You, even when things are hard. I know You are always with me. Amen.

Action Step:

Take some time today to talk to God about your feelings. If you're feeling worried, sad, or scared about something, tell Him all about it. You can pray quietly in your room, or even sit outside and share your heart with God. He cares about what's on your mind and wants to help you.

Day 25 – Jesus is Arrested and Betrayed

Bible Story: Judas and the Soldiers

Scripture: Luke 22:47-53

After Jesus finished praying in the garden, He knew that the time had come. As He walked back to His disciples, He told them that Judas—one of His own followers—was coming to betray Him. And just as Jesus had said, Judas appeared, leading a group of soldiers and temple guards with torches and swords. Judas had made a secret plan with the religious leaders to hand Jesus over to them in exchange for thirty pieces of silver. Now, He had come to do exactly what he had promised.

With a kiss, Judas betrayed Jesus, greeting Him as though He were just a friend. "Greetings, Rabbi!" he said as he approached.

But Jesus knew exactly what was happening. He turned to Judas and asked,

"Judas, are you betraying the Son of Man with a kiss?" The disciples were shocked. They didn't know what to do! One of them, Peter, grabbed a sword and tried to defend Jesus by striking one of the servants of the high priest. But Jesus stopped him, saying, "No more of this!" Then He touched the servant's ear and healed it.

Jesus then spoke to the soldiers and guards, saying, "Am I leading a rebellion, that you have come with swords and clubs? Every day I was with you in the temple courts, and you did not lay a hand on Me. But this is your hour—when darkness reigns." Even though Jesus knew He was going to suffer and die, He didn't fight back. Instead, He allowed Himself to be arrested because He knew it was God's plan to save the world.

Reflection:

Have you ever felt hurt by someone you trusted? Judas was one of Jesus' closest disciples, but he betrayed Jesus. That must have been so hard for Jesus. But even when Jesus was hurt, He didn't seek revenge. He didn't fight back. He knew God's plan was bigger than His own hurt and pain. Just like Jesus, when we're hurt or treated unfairly, we can choose forgiveness instead of anger. Jesus showed us that love is stronger than hate.

Prayer:

Dear Jesus, thank You for showing us how to forgive even when we are hurt. Help me to love others like You love me and to forgive others, even when it's hard. Thank You for being with me no matter what. Amen.

Action Step:

Think of someone who may have hurt you or someone you know. Pray for them, asking God to help you forgive them. You can even write a letter of forgiveness to someone who has hurt you—whether you send it or not, it will help you release that hurt and find peace.

Day 26 – Jesus Stands Before Pilate

Bible Story: Jesus is Put on Trial

Scripture: Matthew 27:11-26

After Jesus was arrested in the garden, He was brought before Pilate, the Roman governor, to stand trial. Pilate was the man who had the power to decide what would happen to Jesus. The religious leaders had accused Jesus of many things, but none of them were true. They were angry because Jesus had claimed to be the Son of God, and He had been teaching the people about God's kingdom instead of following the rules they had set up. As Pilate looked at Jesus, he didn't see any crime that Jesus had committed. He asked Jesus, "Are you the King of the Jews?" Jesus calmly replied, "You have said so." Pilate was confused. He didn't understand why the people were so upset with Jesus. He could see that Jesus was innocent, but the religious leaders kept shouting accusations at Him. Pilate asked Jesus, "Don't you hear the testimony they are bringing against you?" But

Jesus remained silent. Pilate was amazed that Jesus wasn't defending Himself. He knew the leaders wanted to get rid of Jesus because they felt threatened by Him, but Pilate didn't think Jesus deserved to die. The crowd, however, was loud and angry. Pilate had a custom during the Passover festival to release one prisoner to the people—either a criminal or someone who was innocent. Pilate hoped that, when given the choice, the people would choose to set Jesus free, but the religious leaders had a different plan. They stirred up the crowd to ask for the release of Barabbas, a criminal who had been involved in a rebellion. Pilate was shocked and asked the crowd, "Which one do you want me to release to you? Barabbas, or Jesus, who is called the Messiah?" The crowd shouted back, "Barabbas!" Pilate was confused, so he asked again, "What shall I do, then, with Jesus who is called the Messiah?" The crowd screamed, "Crucify Him!" Pilate didn't understand why they wanted to hurt an innocent man, but he saw that the crowd was getting more and more upset. Pilate even tried to reason with them, asking,

"Why? What crime has He committed?" But the crowd just yelled louder, "Crucify Him!" Pilate knew that he couldn't stop the crowd, so he gave in. He washed his hands in front of them and said, "I am innocent of this man's blood. It is your responsibility." He was trying to show that he didn't want to be part of what was happening. But despite his efforts, Pilate ordered Jesus to be scourged (whipped) and then handed over to the soldiers to be crucified.

The crowd had gotten what they wanted. Jesus was going to be crucified, even though He had done nothing wrong. Pilate was trying to stay neutral, but he had failed to stand up for what was right. In the end, he allowed Jesus to be treated unfairly.

Reflection:

Pilate was in a tough spot. He knew Jesus hadn't done anything wrong, but he was afraid of upsetting the crowd, so he gave in. It can be hard to do the right thing when everyone around us is making the wrong choice. But Jesus shows us the importance of standing up for what is right, even if it's hard. When we see someone being treated unfairly, or when we're faced with tough choices, we can follow Jesus' example. We don't have to be afraid to do the right thing. Jesus shows us that God is with us when we choose what's right, even if it's not easy.

Prayer:

Dear Jesus, thank You for showing us how to stand strong and do what is right, even when others are doing the wrong thing. Help me to make the right choices, even when it's hard, and to trust that You are with me no matter what. Thank You for loving me and showing me the way. Amen.

Action Step:

Think of a time when it was hard for you to do the right thing. Talk to God about it and ask for His help to be strong next time. If you see someone else making a tough choice, you can be a good friend by helping them make the right choice, just like Jesus does for us.

Holy Week: Jesus' Journey to the Cross

Day 27 – Good Friday: Jesus Dies on the Cross

Theme of the Day: The Great Sacrifice: Jesus Shows His Love

Bible Story: The Crucifixion

Scripture: Luke 23:33-49

The day had finally come. After a long night of unfair trials, Jesus was led through the streets of Jerusalem to a hill called Golgotha, which means "The Place of the Skull." This was the place where criminals were punished, but Jesus was no criminal. He had done nothing wrong. Still, He carried a heavy cross on His back. The crowd followed behind Him, some of them angry, others weeping for Him. They knew that He had been condemned to die, but many still didn't understand why. At the top of the hill, Jesus was nailed to the cross. The soldiers hammered the nails through His hands and feet, and then they lifted the cross into place. Jesus hung there, bleeding and hurting, in front of the crowd. On either side of Him were two criminals who had also been sentenced to die. As Jesus hung on the cross, the crowd shouted things at Him like, "If You are the King of the Jews, save Yourself!" But Jesus didn't come to save Himself. He came to save us. He loved us so much that He was willing to suffer and die for our sins. While He was on the cross, He prayed for those who were hurting Him. He said, "Father, forgive them, for they do not know what they are doing." Even as people mocked and hurt Him, Jesus still loved them and wanted to forgive them. One of the criminals beside Jesus believed in Him. He said, "Jesus, remember me when You come into Your kingdom." Jesus answered him, "Truly I tell you, today you will be with Me in paradise." Even in the middle of His pain, Jesus showed love and mercy to someone who needed it. At around noon, something strange happened. The sky grew completely dark. It stayed that way for three hours, and during that time, Jesus called out in a loud voice, "Father, into Your hands I commit My spirit!" And with those words, He died. The earth shook, and the curtain in the temple, which separated people from the holy place, was torn in two from top to bottom. A Roman soldier who was standing guard saw everything that happened and said, "Surely, this was the Son of God!" Even the soldiers who had crucified Jesus saw that He was not just an ordinary man. Jesus was the Son of God, and He had done something amazing that day. Jesus' death was the greatest sacrifice ever made. He died because He loved us so much. All the wrong things we have done—the times we have hurt others or turned away from God—were taken away because of His death on the cross. Jesus died so we could be forgiven and have a relationship with God.

Reflection:

On Good Friday, we remember the great sacrifice that Jesus made for us. He didn't deserve to die, but He chose to because He loves us more than we can imagine. Even though it was a sad day, it was also the day that Jesus made a way for us to be close to God again. When we look at the cross, we see how much Jesus loves us and how much He was willing to suffer for us. Just like the criminal on the cross, we can ask Jesus for forgiveness and trust in His love. Jesus doesn't want us to be perfect, but He wants us to come to Him with all our hearts, knowing that He forgives us.

Prayer:

Dear Jesus, thank You for loving me so much that You chose to die on the cross for my sins. I am sorry for the times I've made mistakes, but I'm so thankful that You forgive me. Please help me to love others the way You love me. Thank You for showing me the way to be close to God. Amen.

Action Step:

Take some time today to think about the ways that Jesus has shown His love for you. Draw or write a note to Jesus thanking Him for His sacrifice on the cross. You can also think about someone in your life that you need to forgive, just like Jesus forgave those who hurt Him. Pray for that person, asking God to help you show love and forgiveness.

Day 28 – The Day of Waiting (Holy Saturday)

Theme of the Day: Waiting with Hope: The Promise of New Life

Bible Story: Jesus is Buried

Scripture: Matthew 27:57-66

It was a quiet day, a day of waiting. Jesus had died on the cross, and His body had been taken down from the wooden beams. As the sun set on the day He was crucified, Jesus' friends and followers were filled with sadness and confusion. They didn't understand why this had happened. They had believed that Jesus was the One sent to save them, but now He was gone. Their hearts were heavy with grief.

A man named Joseph of Arimathea, who was a good and righteous man, went to Pontius Pilate, the Roman governor, and asked for Jesus' body. Pilate agreed, and Joseph took the lifeless body of Jesus and wrapped it in a clean linen cloth. Joseph, who had a tomb carved out of a rock, placed Jesus' body inside. It was a tomb meant for him, but now it would hold Jesus. He rolled a large stone in front of the entrance to the tomb to seal it, and it seemed like the story of Jesus had come to an end.

Mary Magdalene and the other Mary, two women who had been following Jesus and loved Him dearly, stayed by the tomb. They watched as the stone was rolled in place, and they wept. They didn't know what would happen next, and they felt so lost without Jesus. The next day, the religious leaders who had plotted against Jesus went to Pilate with a concern. They remembered that Jesus had said He would rise again on the third day. To make sure that no one would steal His body and claim He had come back to life, they asked Pilate to guard the tomb. Pilate agreed, and soldiers were placed at the entrance, securing it with a seal, so that no one could move the stone or tamper with the tomb. On this day, no one knew what was coming next. Everyone was waiting. The followers of Jesus felt hopeless, the religious leaders were trying to make sure everything stayed quiet, and the Roman soldiers stood guard. But in the silence and in the waiting, God was still at work. Even though the tomb was sealed, something powerful was about to happen that would change everything.

Reflection:

Holy Saturday is a day of waiting. After Jesus' death on the cross, His followers were left in grief and confusion. They didn't understand that Jesus' death was only part of the story. Sometimes, we too feel like we are waiting—waiting for answers, waiting for hope, or waiting for things to get better. But even in the quiet and uncertain times, God is still working. On this day, the tomb was sealed, and it seemed like all hope was lost. But God had a plan, and soon, the waiting would be over. Just like the disciples, we may not always understand God's timing, but we can trust that He is always working for our good, even when we can't see it.

Prayer:

Dear God, sometimes I feel like I'm waiting and don't know what's coming next. I know You are always with me, even when things feel quiet or difficult. Please help me to trust You, just like the disciples had to wait for You to show them that You are the risen Savior. Thank You for the hope that You give us. Amen.

Action Step:

Take some time today to sit quietly and think about something you've been waiting for. It could be a prayer that hasn't been answered yet, or something you're hoping for in the future. Write down or draw your feelings about waiting. Remember, just like God had a plan for Jesus, He has a plan for you too. Trust that God is working even when you can't see it. If you feel led, talk to God about your waiting and ask Him to give you hope and peace.

Easter Sunday: Jesus is Alive!

Theme of the Day: The Greatest Miracle: Jesus Is Alive!

Bible Story: The Resurrection

Scripture: Matthew 28:1-10

It had been a long, quiet Saturday. The world felt like it was holding its breath, waiting. Jesus' friends were heartbroken and confused, still mourning the death of their beloved Savior. But then, early Sunday morning, something incredible happened. It was the first day of the week, and the sun was just starting to rise, casting light over the city.

Mary Magdalene and the other Mary—two women who had loved Jesus so much—went to the tomb. They wanted to be near Him, to show Him love, even though they were still deeply sad. As they approached the tomb, suddenly, there was a great earthquake! The ground shook beneath their feet, and an angel of the Lord came down from heaven. He rolled back the heavy stone that was guarding the tomb and sat on it. The angel's face shone like lightning, and his clothes were as white as snow. The guards who had been watching the tomb were so frightened that they fell to the ground like they were dead! But the angel spoke to the women, saying:

"Do not be afraid. I know you are looking for Jesus, who was crucified. He is not here; He has risen, just as He said. Come and see the place where He lay." The women were amazed! They couldn't believe what they were hearing. Jesus, their Savior, was alive! The angel then told them to go quickly and tell Jesus' disciples that He had risen from the dead and was going ahead of them into Galilee. They would see Him there! As the women hurried away from the tomb, their hearts were filled with joy and excitement. But suddenly, Jesus met them on the road! He greeted them and said, "Greetings!" The women fell to their knees, worshiping Him. They couldn't believe their eyes! It was truly Jesus, and He was alive! Jesus spoke to them, saying, "Do not be afraid. Go and tell my brothers to go to Galilee; there they will see me." The women were so filled with joy that they ran to tell the disciples the most amazing news in the world—Jesus had risen from the dead!

Reflection:

Easter is the most exciting day for Christians because it celebrates the day when Jesus defeated death and came back to life! Imagine the joy and excitement the women must have felt when they realized Jesus was alive again. It wasn't just a happy surprise—it was the greatest miracle the world has ever seen. Jesus had promised He would rise, and He did!

When Jesus rose from the dead, it showed that God always keeps His promises. He promised that Jesus would rise, and He did. The resurrection means that we have hope for eternal life with God, no matter what happens on Earth. Jesus' victory over death shows us that nothing is impossible for God. Because of what Jesus did, we can have a relationship with Him and look forward to eternal life in Heaven. Just like the women ran to share the good news with others, we can share the joy of Jesus' resurrection with the people around us. Easter reminds us that Jesus is alive, and that changes everything!

Prayer:

Dear Jesus, thank You for the wonderful gift of life and for rising from the dead to give us hope! Thank You for keeping Your promises. Please help me to remember that You are always with me, even when things are hard. I want to share Your love and joy with everyone I meet. Thank You for loving me so much. Amen.

Action Step:

Celebrate the new life we have in Jesus! Take a moment today to think about the joy and excitement of Easter. You can celebrate by drawing a picture of the empty tomb with the stone rolled away, or you could create a fun card or poster that says, "Jesus is alive!" Share your picture or card with someone to spread the good news. Remember, just like the women in the story, we have the wonderful opportunity to tell others about Jesus and how He's alive forever!

Conclusion

Walking with Jesus Every Day

Congratulations! You've come to the end of this special journey through the season of Lent. Throughout these days, we've learned so much about how much God loves us, how Jesus taught us, and how He gave His life for us. But the best part? Jesus is still with us today!

Just like the disciples walked with Jesus, we can walk with Him too—every day of our lives. He is always near us, helping us, guiding us, and loving us. Whether we are feeling happy, sad, or confused, Jesus is there to listen and be our friend.

This journey doesn't end here. Every day is an opportunity to grow closer to Jesus. He wants us to love others, share His message of hope, and be kind like He was. The lessons we've learned in these 28 days are like seeds that God plants in our hearts, and just like a seed grows into a beautiful tree, our faith can grow stronger and stronger each day.

So remember, Easter isn't just a day we celebrate once a year—it's a reminder that Jesus is alive and living in us all the time. His love never ends, and He is always ready to walk with us through every day of our lives.

As we go forward, let's keep Jesus close, just like we learned about Him in this devotional. And let's be ready to share the good news with everyone we meet, just like the women who went to tell the disciples that Jesus was alive.

Thank you for walking this journey with Jesus. May you continue to grow in His love and know that He is always with you, every step of the way.

With Jesus in our hearts, the journey of faith never ends!

Bonus Chapter

Activities to Keep Following Jesus After Lent

As we finish our special journey through Lent, remember that following Jesus is something we can do every day! Lent was just the beginning of our adventure with Him, and now, we get to keep walking with Jesus every day of our lives. Here are some fun ways to keep growing in faith and following Jesus, even after Lent is over!

1. **Keep a "Jesus Journal"**

One of the best ways to stay close to Jesus is by writing down your thoughts and prayers. You can start a "Jesus Journal" where you write about what you're learning, the ways you see God working in your life, and the things you're thankful for. This will help you remember how Jesus is always with you and how He's changing your heart.

Activity Tip: If you like drawing, you can add pictures to your journal too! Draw things that remind you of God's love, like hearts, crosses, or even scenes from the Bible stories you've learned about.

2. Create a "Good News" Poster

Jesus' love is something we can't keep to ourselves! Just like the women who ran to tell the disciples that Jesus was alive, we can share the good news with our friends and family too. You can create a "Good News" poster with pictures or words that show how happy you are that Jesus is alive and with us forever.

Activity Tip: Use bright colors, stickers, and fun designs to make your poster colorful and joyful. Then, put it somewhere everyone can see, like on your door or the fridge, to remind you and your family of God's love!

3. **Pray for Others**

One way to keep following Jesus is to pray for the people around you. Jesus always cared about others, and He wants us to do the same. You can make a "Prayer Chain" where you and your family write down the names of people or things you want to pray for, then hang them up on a wall or put them in a special box. Every time you pray, you can pull one name out and pray for that person or situation.

Activity Tip: You can also make a "Blessing Jar" where everyone writes down a prayer for someone, and then take turns reading them out loud at dinner or bedtime!

Manufactured by Amazon.ca
Bolton, ON

44159155R00066